BICYCLE RACING

BY

Nancy J. Nielsen

PUBLISHED BY

CRESTWOOD HOUSE

Mankato, MN, U.S.A.

CIP

LIBRARY OF CONGRESS CATALOGING IN PUBLICATION DATA

Nielsen, Nancy J.
   Bicycle racing.
   (Super-Charged!)
   Includes index.
   SUMMARY: Describes different types of bicycle races, including track and road races,
BMX racing, and mountain biking, the variety of bicycles used, and racing strategies.
   1. Bicycle racing — Juvenile literature.   [1. Bicycle racing]   I. Title.
GV1049.N475   1988   796.6   87-30489
ISBN 0-89686-361-1

International Standard Book Number:	Library of Congress Catalog Card Number:
0-89686-361-1	87-30489

CREDITS

Cover: Focus West: (Robert Beck)
Reuter/Bettmann Newsphotos: 4
The Bettmann Archives: 8, 9, 11
Focus West: (Dave Black) 13, 14, 15, 23; (Stephen Dunn) 26-27
SIPA Sports/Focus West: 40, 41, 42
Globe Photos, Inc.: (Tony Guzewicz) 18-19; (Rebecca Twig) 37
FPG International: (John Terence Turner) 6-7, 16-17, 21; (Jeffrey Sylvester) 24-25;
(Ron Whitby) 29; (David Lissy) 34
Third Coast Stock Source: (William Meyer) 30-31, 44
Frozen Images: (Kurt Mitchell) 32

Produced by Carnival Enterprises.

CRESTWOOD HOUSE

Box 3427, Mankato, MN, U.S.A. 56002

TABLE OF CONTENTS

A GRUELING SPORT

It was a race 23 days and 2,542 miles (4,090 kilometers) long. Pedaling up to six hours a day in mountainous French terrain, American Greg LeMond was determined to win the most difficult bicycle race in the world, the Tour de France.

Each day Greg attached special racing shoes to the pedals of his lightweight speed bike and went head-to-head with the best cyclists in the world. He needed his iron-strong thigh muscles and the special techniques he had carefully learned. Each night he was exhausted.

He struggled harder and harder to keep ahead of the pack of hungry cyclists. One mistake and he could end up in the ditch. One fall and his career could be over.

Traveling at speeds up to 60 miles per hour (mph) or 96 kilometers per hour (km/h), Greg did not give up. Finally the grueling race was over. His times for each day's distance were added together. He had finished three minutes and ten seconds ahead of his nearest rival.

Greg LeMond, from Reno, Nevada, was the first American ever to win the Tour de France. All his hard work and endurance had paid off!

Bicycle racing champion Greg LeMond (right) became the first American to win the famous Tour de France.

5

The sensation of bicycle riding is one-of-a-kind.

RACERS AND RIDERS

Many people all over the world ride bicycles. Some ride for transportation. Others ride for fun—and some people are bicycle racers.

Racers train hard, ride lightweight racing bikes, and

learn special techniques that help them go fast. They are not cycling to go from one place to the next. They are racing to be the fastest!

A racer cannot win unless he is determined and in shape. Also, he must work with a smooth and durable bicycle, a machine to help him be the best.

The first bicycles were called Hobby-Horses, and they had no brakes.

A HISTORY OF BICYCLES

The first bicycle was invented in Europe in the late 1700's. It was called a Hobby-Horse, and it had no pedals. Riders used their feet to push off the ground. Later a Scotsman devised a system of foot levers to make his Hobby-Horse go faster. His bike could travel up to 14 mph (22 km/h).

In the mid-1800's, a new bicycle was invented—

The Ordinary, with its big front wheel, was designed to make pedaling easier.

The Boneshaker. It had pedals attached to the front wheel. Cyclists had to lean backwards to pedal. Then an inventor decided to put the rider on top of the front wheel. That provided more leverage for pedaling. The Ordinary, a bicycle with a huge front wheel and a small back wheel, traveled about 15 mph (24 km/h).

But the Ordinary was a dangerous bike. It was hard to mount, and a fall could mean disaster! A safer bicycle was needed.

Finally in the late 1800's, the Safety bicycle was invented. It had two wheels of the same size, and the back wheel was powered with a chain and sprocket attached to pedals. It was easier to steer and gave a steadier ride. Bicycle racing soon became popular and was included in the modern Olympic Games in 1896.

EARLY AMERICAN RACERS

The first World Amateur Sprint Champion was an American named Arthur Zimmerman. Marshall Taylor, a black American, was the World Professional Sprint Champion in 1899.

But one of America's greatest heroes in the early 1900's was a bicyclist named Frank Kramer. He was the U.S. professional champion in bicycle racing from 1901 to 1916. He also won in 1918 and again in 1921 (when he was 41 years old).

The New York Times in 1922 called Kramer's record "one of amazing endurance and stamina, not to mention success. (His record is) one of the most marvelous in athletic history."

During Kramer's time, Americans were the best bicycle racers in the world. Many racers from other countries came to the U.S. just to beat Kramer. Still, Kramer managed to stay on top.

America was proud of Kramer. Thousands of fans would jam the stands to watch him race. One of his

An early bicycle race.

fans was young Jack Simes.

Simes remembers going with his father in 1922 when he was eight years old to watch Kramer race. Soon he began racing bicycles himself. Fourteen years later, he became America's Amateur Road Cycling Champion.

Now in his 70's, Simes remembers Kramer as his hero. "I don't care what anybody says," Simes recalls. "There's never been an athlete, before or since, that could hold a candle to Frank Kramer."

Unfortunately, bicycle racing faded during the 1930's as a spectator sport in America. Some people think this is because Americans were caught up with the automobile. They began to think of bicycles as only for children. Many of the racing tracks sat unused and most were destroyed. Bicycle racing did not become popular in America again until the 1970's.

In Europe, however, people continued to ride bicycles because cars were very expensive. Bicycle racing remained an important sport. Today, many races are shown on television. They are as popular in Europe as the Super Bowl is in America!

TRACK RACING

Both Kramer and Simes raced on velodromes. A velodrome is a race track built for bicycle racing. Track races are easier to watch than road races. Up to 20,000 people can crowd into the bleachers surrounding the tracks to watch bicycle races.

The oval-shaped velodromes are 1/10 to 1/3 of a mile (1/2 of a kilometer) around. They can be built indoors or outdoors. Indoor tracks are usually made of wood. Outdoor velodromes are often made from concrete or cement. The tracks are "banked." This

These racers are competing in a modern velodrome, a concrete track with banked turns.

means the track slopes upward, especially on the ends, to make turning easier. The longer stretches of track that join the ends together are called "straightaways."

Racing on a track can be dangerous because racers ride so close together. Quick reflexes are needed. If a rider should fall, other riders must dodge around him or they may all end up in a heap. It's easy to lock handlebars or slip against another racer during a heated event.

All bicycle racers wear helmets for protection.

Track racing bicycles are very lightweight. They can weigh as little as 11 pounds (5 kilograms) because they have no fenders, no gear shifts—not even any brakes! Racers place a gloved hand on the front tire to help them slow down and stop.

Racers wear special clothing that's comfortable and that helps cut down on wind resistance. Both the shirt, called a jersey, and racing shorts are tight-fitting. They are made of silk or another smooth material. A racer wears a helmet to protect his head in case of a crash.

Biking shoes have a stiff sole so they cannot bend. They are designed to clip directly onto the pedals to keep a racer's feet in position.

Though it seems strange, the winner of a track race

The banked curves of a velodrome increase the speed of a race.

Modern racing cycles are made of lightweight materials to improve speed.

16

Riders often follow each other closely to take advantage of slipstreaming.

is often not the one that races in front. That's because the first racer must "break" the wind. They are working harder and can tire quickly. Cyclists traveling just behind the first rider can ride in the draft he creates. Then they don't have to work as hard.

Cyclists often try to ride in someone else's draft (sometimes called "slipstreaming") until the race is almost over. Then, at the last moment, they try to sprint ahead. The racer who crosses the finish line first is the winner!

TRACK EVENTS

Many different kinds of races are held on tracks. A "mass start" event is the simplest kind. All the racers start from the same place at the same time. The first rider to cross the finish line after a certain number of laps is the winner.

Long races are made more interesting by offering prizes within the race called "primes." For example, racers who finish a certain portion of the race first are awarded points. The racer with the most points at the end of the race is the winner.

Another race is the "miss-and-out." The last person to cross the finish line on each lap is taken out of the race. Soon there are only four, then three, then two racers left to compete. The winner is the one who crosses the finish line first during the last lap.

Specialized events such as the world championships or the Olympics include a race called the "time trial." Each racer rides one kilometer (about 5/8 of a mile) by himself. He has no one to compete with, no opponent to sit in his draft. It is a personal race against the clock. The cyclist with the fastest time wins.

In a "matched sprint," two to four riders race against each other. The first racer to cross the finish line is the winner. Winners later race the winners from other sprints until the best two racers compete against each other during the finals.

During team races, teammates take turns riding the

Team competition is a regular feature of velodome cycle racing.

laps. This way, individual team members can race at their top speed and then have a chance to rest before they must race again. Most team races are an hour or two long. The team that covers the most laps during that time is the winner.

Sometimes racers start at opposite sides of the track and try to overtake one another. Both individuals and teams compete in these races, called "pursuit races." If they are unable to overtake the other, the individual or team with the fastest time wins.

In a "team pursuit," the four team members take turns riding in front while the other riders stay behind in the slipstream. The teammates ride close together. Only inches separate the bicycles from each other. The third member of the team is the one that is timed as he crosses the finish line.

An interesting race popular in Europe is the "motorpace." Cyclists travel behind a motorcycle which breaks the wind and provides them with a draft. Because they do not have to battle against the wind, motorpace racers can sometimes travel 50 mph (80 km/h).

ROAD RACING

A road race is any race that takes place on a street or highway instead of a velodrome. City streets are often blocked off and used for these races. Sometimes cyclists must even share roads or highways with cars.

Road bicycles are lightweight like track bicycles. But road bikes are ridden over longer and more varying terrain and need additional equipment.

Road bicycles are equipped with gears which provide from five to fifteen different speeds. The most common road bike is the 12-speed. Cyclists can shift from one gear to the next with the help of a "derailleur," which moves the bicycle chain from one gear to another.

The mass start of a long road race resembles a traffic jam!

Riders preparing for the start of a long race.

SOMERSET COUNTY PARK COMM

25

Long, uphill climbs are not unusual in some road races.

Road racers must be able to climb up and down hills smoothly. When they come to a difficult hill, they shift down into an easier gear. This makes it possible for them to cycle at the same pace as they travel up the hill. When they come to a downhill, racers shift into a higher gear, which helps them pedal harder and gain more mileage.

Road bikes must also be equipped with brakes. It would not be safe for cyclists to travel at fast speeds on roads without a way of stopping.

Road cyclists dress just like track racers. But one difference is that their jerseys have large pockets so they can carry food. Helmets protect them in case of a fall.

ROAD EVENTS

There are three different kinds of road racing events—the time trial, mass starts, and stage races.

As in track racing, the time trial is a race against the clock. Racers start separately, usually one minute apart. But time trial road races are much longer than the track time trial. The most common is 25 miles (40 kilometers), but some are as long as 100 miles (160 kilometers).

During a mass start race, hundreds of racers start at the same time. Criteriums and road races are the two different kinds of mass starts.

The criterium is typically held on city streets. Racers travel the course for many laps until they have covered the distance, usually from 25 to 75 miles. Primes are offered to make the race more interesting. The test for racers during a criterium is to stay upright on a crowded course and be able to handle fast speeds around difficult corners.

A criterium racer must use special tactics, such as riding in someone else's slipstream. Another tactic, called the "breakaway," occurs when a group of pedalers try to get ahead of all the others early in the race. Breakaway cyclists pedal aggressively and fight their way to the front of the pack. In the meantime, teammates help them by blocking the other cyclists.

Opponents in a breakaway may actually help each other maintain their lead at first. They do this by

A race held on city streets is called a criterium.

taking turns breaking the wind for each other until they are far ahead of the other contestants.

Road races are longer than criteriums and are often held on hilly country roads. They cover 100 miles (160 kilometers) or more. Sometimes they are organized as "handicap" races. Beginners start first and the more experienced bicyclists must catch and overtake them.

It's thrilling to see a pack of cyclists rushing by.

The excitement of a road race is enhanced by the changing landscape.

This race is one of endurance. Riders become spread out over the course. They must know how to climb hills and how to conserve energy. Many are forced to drop out because of exhaustion or mechanical problems. Support vans follow the cyclists to help them repair their bikes or change a flat tire.

The stage race is considered the most challenging of all cycle races. It consists of many smaller races held one after the other. Racers may perform in a time trial one day, and then pedal 50 or 100 miles (80 to 160 kilometers) in a road race the next day. During the course of the race, they may go against each other more than once in criterium races. The cyclist who has the best overall time when all the stages are completed is the winner.

AMERICAN ROAD RACES

Many road races are held each year in the United States and in other countries around the world. The winners of professional races receive prize money. Racers are often sponsored by businesses who pay them to ride for their team. Greg LeMond is the highest paid bicyclist in the world. He makes more than $1 million a year!

One of America's most important road races is the Coors International Bicycle Classic, a 15-day stage race. The race first attracted world competitors when

A winner raises her fist in victory.

Frenchman Bernard Hinault raced alongside teammate and 1985 winner Greg LeMond.

1985 is also the first year the race took place in areas outside of the state of Colorado. Racers started with a criterium in San Francisco, California. Next they competed in a road race from Sonoma to Sacramento. Then they crossed over into Nevada, Greg's home state, before finishing in the race's birthplace, Boulder, Colorado.

Hinault raced in the Classic again in 1986 along with dozens of other international racers. There he grabbed a win away from Greg before retiring later that year.

THE TOUR DE FRANCE

When it comes to road races, there is none to compare with the Tour de France. The Tour de France is an international 22-stage race that takes place each year in June. Millions of people turn out to watch as racers pass through many small French villages.

The race is also shown overseas on TV. Newspapers around the world cover the race. It is the most famous and challenging of all bicycle races.

The lead rider in the Tour wears a yellow jersey. The yellow color is often transferred between several riders before the race is finally over.

EDDIE MERCKX, AN INTERNATIONAL STAR

Many people consider Eddie Merckx of Belgium to be the best road racer ever. Merckx dominated bicycle racing from the mid-1960's to the mid-1970's. He won the Tour de France five times. He set a world one-hour record at 30 mph (49 km/h). He has won nearly every major road event at least once, for a total of more than 450 wins!

Competition against Merckx, especially among Europeans, was very stiff. Still, Merckx kept winning until he retired in 1976. He had won so many races over such a long period of time that he had become a millionaire!

WOMEN IN RACING

The Coors International Bicycle Classic is the top race for women. Each year it attracts more and more international competitors.

There is also a famous women-only race in the United States. It's the Ore-Ida Women's Challenge, an eight-stage race held each summer in Idaho. Large groups of women compete in many of the other races held each year in this country.

1984 was the first year women raced in the famous Tour de France. They cycled shorter distances on the same course as the men but had the same celebrity status. The 1984 women's winner was an American, Marianne Martin.

Jeannie Longo of France placed first among women

Rebecca Twigg Whitehead was one of America's standouts during the 1984 Olympic Games.

in the 1986 and 1987 tours. She also won the 1986 World Championship Road Race. She is considered the No. 1 woman cyclist in the world today.

American road racers Connie Carpenter-Phinney and Rebecca Twigg Whitehead were highly ranked amateurs who won big in the 1984 Olympics. Connie won a gold medal when she beat Rebecca by a couple of inches.

Women cyclists in the U.S. have long pushed for more races and more challenging courses for women. For example, the U.S. women's cycling team lobbied to have women's bicycling included in the Pan American Games. Because of their efforts, women cyclists first participated in the Games in 1987.

MOUNTAIN BIKING

Both track and road racing challenge all cyclists. Another type of challenge is offered by the harsh, bumpy, rough terrain of mountain biking!

Mountain bikes are rugged bikes with straight handlebars and heavy-duty brakes. They have fat, knobby tires built to withstand punishment from rocks, sticks, and loose gravel. Riders daringly leave the roads behind and travel on hiking or skiing wilderness trails.

Mountain bikers ride with more variables than road racers. They must learn to watch for the unexpected — slippery surfaces, tree roots, sudden jumps, and plunges. Sometimes they have to get off their bikes and carry them over fallen trees!

Mountain bikes are equipped with 12 to 18 speeds, providing the low gears necessary to climb steep, rocky grades. The bikes were first sold in 1979 and are becoming very popular in America. In 1986, one out of every four bicycles sold was a mountain bike.

National championships are often held on a rugged 18-mile (29-kilometer) course near Boulder, Colorado. Other well-known races include the Whiskeytown Downhill held in Redding, California, and the Race Around the Base at Mount Bachelor, Oregon.

Mountain bikers are tough. Jungle Jon is an ex-New York City bicycle messenger. Tony Herich from New Mexico is a cowboy who herds cattle with his mountain bike! Another moutain biker is Michael Hiltner who was a member of two Olympic bicycling teams before he dropped out of 10-speed racing in favor of mountain biking.

Jacquie Phelan, the top woman in mountain biking, started in 10-speed racing before switching over to mountain biking. She likes the individuality of mountain biking where teamwork is not necessary.

"It's perfectly okay to train alone," she said, "because you'll be alone in the races, except at the start."

BMX RACING

The sport of BMX grew out of cross-country motorcycle racing which is called "motocross." The abbreviation for motocross is "MX." BMX, then, stands for "bicycle motocross."

BMX racers prefer the excitement of a track sport.

BMX racing requires a different set of skills…

BMX races include daring stunts, special tactics for winning close races, and crowds of spectators.

The BMX bike is a strong, lightweight bike, much smaller than a 10-speed. Just like track racing bicycles, they have no gears. The frame and wheel rims are built from sturdier materials than other bikes, and the wheel rims have more spokes. They also have no

... and a bike with its own special modifications.

fenders, chainguards, or kickstands.

Unlike the traditional velodromes, BMX tracks are carved out of the dirt. They include many difficult hairpin turns and are steeply banked. Races begin from a starting gate, usually the top of a hill to help racers gather speed quickly. Most courses contain trick obstacles such as sudden dips, bumps, and even jumps.

BMX races are typically held on tough, hilly courses made from mud and gravel.

Preparation is an important part of BMX racing. Contestants practice the course until they know it well and develop a strategy. They must also wear protective clothing, including elbow and knee pads, special boots, gloves, and helmets.

Racers fight each other for the lead. They lean their bicycles into a turn to gain more speed. They can use their legs or bicycles to block other racers who try to pass them. Sometimes racers lose control and take a spill. Unless they get hurt, they hop back on their bikes and finish the race.

"It gets really physical," said Eric Rupe, a national champion BMX racer. "You have to be tough." Though he's been racing over 10 years, the only injury Eric has suffered is a sprained ankle.

HOW RACES ARE ORGANIZED

Local bicycle clubs exist throughout the country. Most of these clubs belong to the United States Cycling Federation (USCF). USCF races are organized on the local, state, regional, national, and international level.

People who wish to race in USCF races must first apply for a license. It comes with a rulebook and a subscription to the USCF magazine which includes a calendar of races.

Riders compete according to gender and age: midget (8-11), junior (15-17), senior (ages 18 and older), and veterans (over 40).

Professional racers in America are governed by the Professional Racing Organization of America. The international bicycling organization has two branches for professional and amateur racers.

Racers who are interested in competing in the Olympics, held every four years, must still be amateurs. The Olympics include a road race, a team time trial, sprint and individual races, and a team pursuit.

GETTING STARTED

If you've been riding a bicycle for a number of years and think you might want to start racing, the best thing to do is join a local bicycling club. They can show you how to join the USCF.

Club activities may include meetings, training rides, coaching, and racing. These activities will help prepare you for your first USCF race.

If your community has a velodrome, you may want to attend a few races and then contact the track for more information. Some velodromes have full-time managers who conduct regular classes on track racing. Velodromes generally schedule weekly races during the bicycle season (early April to September).

Whether you decide to join a bicycle club, or simply watch a track event, bicycle racing will show you excitement!

Bike racing may be the sport for you!

FOR MORE INFORMATION

For more information on bicycle racing, write to:
United States Cycling Federation
Box 669
Wall Street Station
New York, NY 10005

GLOSSARY/INDEX

BANKING 12, 41 — *The upward tilt or slope of a bicycle race track which helps riders take the turns faster without slipping.*

BMX 39, 40, 41, 42, 43 — *Abbreviation for "bicycle motocross."*

BREAKAWAY 28 — *A group of riders that leaves the main group of racers behind.*

CHAIN 10, 22 — *A circular mechanism made from flexible pieces of metal which connects the pedals of a bicycle to the derailleur (gears).*

CRITERIUM 28, 29, 33, 34 — *A road event in which riders complete many laps of a closed course.*

DERAILLEUR 22 — *A mechanical device used to shift the chain from one gear to another.*

DRAFTING 18, 19, 20, 22 — *Being protected from the wind by riding close behind another rider. This allows the rider in the rear to maintain the same speed with less physical effort.*

GEARS 14, 22, 26, 38, 40 — *A system of toothed wheels of different sizes attached to the chain of a speed bicycle. Each wheel, when caught by the chain, moves the bicycle a different distance.*

HANDICAP 29 — *An event in which groups of riders start at different intervals to give the slower riders an earlier start.*

JERSEY 15, 27, 35 — *A racing shirt made from silk or nylon.*

47

GLOSSARY/INDEX

MASS START 20, 28 — *An event in which all riders start at the same time and place.*

MISS-AND-OUT 20 — *A track event in which the last rider over the line on each lap is removed from the race.*

MOTOCROSS 39 — *Cross-country motorcycle racing.*

MOTORPACE 22 — *A track event in which a racer rides in the slipstream of a motorcycle.*

PRIMES 20, 28 — *Points or prizes within a race.*

PURSUIT RACES 21, 22, 45 — *A track event in which racers start at opposite ends of the track and try to overtake one another.*

SLIPSTREAM 19, 22, 28 — *The area of least wind resistance right behind another rider.*

SPRINT 10, 19, 20, 45 — *A race in which a rider travels as fast as possible throughout the entire race.*

SPROCKET 10 — *One of the toothed wheels to which a bicycle chain is connected.*

STAGE RACE 28, 33, 35, 36 — *A road event which consists of several different kinds of races. The rider who completes all of them in the least amount of time wins.*

STRAIGHTAWAYS 13 — *The straight sections of a racing track.*

TIME TRIAL 20, 28, 33, 45 — *An event in which individuals or teams start separately and are clocked for the fastest time.*

VELODROME 12, 22, 45 — *An indoor or outdoor oval shaped race track.*